# Table of Contents

What is Snow? 3

Photo Glossary 15

Index 16

About the Author 16

# Can you find these words?

| blizzard | freeze |
| --- | --- |
| snowflake | storm |

# What is Snow?

freeze

The sky is cold. Wet drops **freeze**.

Drops stick to each other. They grow.

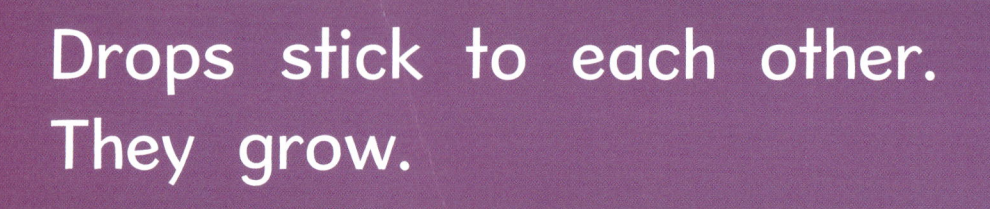

They make shapes.

# A **snowflake** is born!

snowflake

7

Flakes get heavy.

They fall.

9

# Lots of snow!

A **storm!**

storm

# Snow and wind!

blizzard

A blizzard!

# Did you find these words?

Snow and wind! A **blizzard**!

The sky is cold. Wet drops **freeze**.

A **snowflake** is born!

Lots of snow. A **storm**!

# Photo Glossary

**blizzard** (BLIZ-urd): A snowstorm with lots of snow and wind.

**freeze** (freez): To turn to ice.

**snowflake** (SNOH-flake): A crystal of snow.

**storm** (storm): Lots of snow or rain.

# Index

blizzard 13
cold 3
freeze 3

sky 3
storm 11
wind 12

## About the Author

Tammy Brown writes books and teaches teachers how to teach their students to read. She loves to look at snow from inside the house where it is warm and cozy!

© 2019 Rourke Educational Media

All rights reserved. No part of this book may be reproduced or utilized in any form or by any means, electronic or mechanical including photocopying, recording, or by any information storage and retrieval system without permission in writing from the publisher.

www.rourkeeducationalmedia.com

PHOTO CREDITS: Cover: Imgorthand; p. 2,12,14,15: ©Dmitriy Kochergin; p. 2,3,14,15: ©Syntheticmessiah; p. 2,6,14,15: ©ch123; p. 2,10,14,15: ©JANIFEST; p. 4: ©Warchi; p. 8: ©ArtMarie

Edited by: Keli Sipperley
Cover design by: Kathy Walsh
Interior design by: Rhea Magaro-Wallace

**Library of Congress PCN Data**
What is Snow? / Tammy Brown
(I Know)
ISBN (hard cover)(alk. paper) 978-1-64156-170-9
ISBN (soft cover) 978-1-64156-226-3
ISBN (e-Book) 978-1-64156-279-9
Library of Congress Control Number: 2017957780

Printed in the United States of America, North Mankato, Minnesota